Renew Your Mind and Be Blessed

Melvina Harrison

iUniverse, Inc.
New York   Bloomington

Renew Your Mind and Be Blessed

iUniverse books may be ordered through booksellers or by contacting:

iUniverse
1663 Liberty Drive
Bloomington, IN 47403
www.iuniverse.com
1-800-Authors (1-800-288-4677)

Because of the dynamic nature of the Internet, any Web addresses or links contained in this book may have changed since publication and may no longer be valid.

ISBN: 978-1-4401-1510-3 (pbk)
ISBN: 978-1-4401-1511-0 (ebk)

Printed in the United States of America

iUniverse rev. date: 12/10/2009

INTRODUCTION

Do you want to have Joy and not be confused with fear, worry, and negative thoughts? Then allow the Lord to "Renew Your Mind", so that you can receive all the Blessings that God has promised you. God has promised that you will be blessed in the city, blessed on your job, blessed in your home, and every thing you touch will be blessed. He also promised that you would be the head and not the tail; you would be above and not beneath; your children will be blessed and your children's children will be blessed. However to accomplish this you must "Renew your Mind" to God's way of thinking; and God's way of doing things. By doing this you must follow the instructions given by God.

As you read this book set aside time to meditate on the word of God as these pages saturate your mind for renewal. If you follow God's plan of instruction for your life, you will be happier, you will be healthier, you will live longer, and you will be successful in every area of your life.

Receive all the blessings that have been promised by God. Renew you mind and be Blessed today!

Contents

Get Into Position to Be Blessed!!

Deuteronomy 28:11-13 (New King James Version)

11 And the LORD will grant you plenty of goods, in the fruit of your body, in the increase of your livestock, and in the produce of your ground, in the land of which the LORD swore to your fathers to give you. 12 The LORD will open to you His good treasure, the heavens, to give the rain to your land in its season, and to bless all the work of your hand. You shall lend to many nations, but you shall not borrow. 13 And the LORD will make you the head and not the tail; you shall be above only, and not be beneath, if you heed the commandments of the LORD your God, which I command you today, and are careful to observe them.

Have you ever seen people get into position to run a race? Whether it was on television, while watching the Olympics or at a high school marathon. The first thing they are told to do before the whistle blows is to "Get into Position".   However, before these runners begin to run, they must prepare themselves. They prepare themselves with the:

- ➢ Proper Training
- ➢ Proper Nutrition
- ➢ Proper Mentoring or Coaching
- ➢ Proper Rest and
- ➢ Proper Attitude.

That's what God want us to do is to "Get into Position to be Blessed", so that we can be a "Blessing to others". The bible says in *John 15:7. If you abide in Me, and My words abide in you, you will ask what you desire, and it shall be done for you.* God wants us to prosper. He wants us to be blessed, so that we can bless other people.   *3 John 1:2 says, Beloved, I pray that you may prosper in all things and be in health, just as your soul prospers.*

God has placed in us a desire to prosper and receive all the riches he has in store for us. But there are several things we must do in order to accomplish it.

1. Believe It. You are already blessed, you just have to believe it in order to receive it. We can even go a step further and say: Believe it, See it, and Receive it!

Mark 11:24 Therefore I say unto you, What things soever ye desire, when ye pray, believe that ye receive them, and ye shall have them.

2. See it. See yourself with it. Have a vision for it and Visualize it. Not only see the vision, but see from the vision. If you want a new house. What does it look like? Who's living there with you? As you walk into the house, what do you see? And what do you smell?

"Without a vision, the People Perish".

3. What is your reason for wanting more than enough? Do you want to bless others? Give to the Poor? Bless you Family?

Proverbs 13:22 A good man leaves an inheritance to his children's children, But the wealth of the sinner is stored up for the righteous.

4. Surround yourself around knowledgeable people. Have a mentor, someone who can help you become successful.

➤ Learn about Investments
➤ Money Market accounts
➤ Investing in Real Estate
➤ Get into the 401K on your job.

5. Finally, Give to Others. God loves a cheerful giver, so give to those who are less fortunate than you. ***Luke 6:38 Give, and it shall be given unto you; good measure, pressed down, and shaken together, and running over, shall men give into your bosom. For with the same measure that ye mete withal it shall be measured to you again.***

2 Corinthians 9: 6 But this I say: He who sows sparingly will also reap sparingly, and he who sows bountifully will also reap bountifully. 7 So let each one give as he purposes in his heart, not grudgingly or of necessity; for God loves a cheerful giver.

Melvina Harrison

QUESTIONS FOR REFLECTION

1.   *What are some ways you can get into Position to be Blessed?*

2.   *What are your Goals, Dreams and Aspirations? Write it down.*

3.   *Visualize your success.*

RENEW YOUR MIND AND BE BLESSED

Rom 12:2 And be not conformed to this world: but be ye transformed by the renewing of your mind...... (KJV)

The mind controls every aspect of the body. Consequently, the body does exactly what the mind tells it to do. Yes, the mind controls the body, soul, and spirit. We all know that the brain is the central function of all movement and controls our physiological functions; however, the mind controls all of our mental functions, as well. Some people have clear minds, dirty minds, depressed minds, confused minds, and sick minds. Nevertheless, the mind controls your whole being.

The bible says, "To renew your mind." And our minds are renewed when we are saturated with the word of God. When engrossed with a Positive mindset, we can accomplish anything our mind tells us to.

Actually, our mindset determines our attitude about life, about ourselves, and about other people.

Many times our mind can give us false preconceived notions about our sense of identity and in many cases, may cause an attitude of guilt, worthlessness, and inferiority.

We can also develop a negative mindset about other people, fears of self consciousness, anger, hatred, bitterness, jealousy, and unforgiveness.

The mind can even play tricks on us by stimulating beliefs that are untrue. There is a story of a man who was accidentally locked in a refrigerator compartment of a truck and though the refrigerated unit was broken, his mind told him that the refrigerator's freezer unit was getting colder and colder, until finally, he froze to death in that broken compartment. The next day when the refrigerator unit was opened, people were surprised to see him dead because they knew there was enough air for him to survive plus the temperature within the unit was a mere 72 degrees.

It's amazing what our minds do to stimulate our thoughts either negatively or positively. But our minds should be set on God, because God can restore our minds and give us perfect peace and tranquility. The Bible says, "For to be carnally minded is death, but to be spiritually minded is life and peace."

The Bible also says in the following scriptures:

Phil. 4:8 - "Whatever is true, right, pure...let your mind dwell on these things..."

Col. 3:2 - "Set your mind on things above..."

How can the mind be renewed to develop Godly *attitudes*?

1. ***Establish an attitude***, which is consistent with God's character - purity, righteousness, love, joy.

2. ***Establish an attitude of newness.*** Be made new again.

   Rom. 14:5 - "Let each man be fully convinced in his own mind."

3. ***Discipline yourself*** for the purpose of godliness and create a new attitude.

Other ways to have a new attitude or a good frame of mine:

Choose your Attitude.

Decide if you want to a have a positive or negative one. We all have choices.

Pray.

Pray to God for a new attitude because "Any man be in Christ is a new creature..."

Decide.

Make a conscience decision to have a Godly life and Godly attitude because "Your attitude can make you or break you."

Finally, "Change your way of thinking and the direct result will be the renewal of your mind." - Rom. 12:2

Melvina Harrison

THE POWER OF THE TONGUE!!!

"Out of the same mouth proceedeth Blessing and cursing. My Brethren, these things ought not to be so" -James 3:10

The tongue can be your best friend or your worst enemy. Your words, your dreams, and your thoughts have the power to create all conditions in your life. What you speak about, you can bring about.

"Death and Life are in the power of the tongue: and they that love it shall eat the fruit thereof." Proverbs 18:21

If you keep saying you can't stand your job, you might lose your job.

If you keep saying you can't stand your body, your body can become sick.

If you keep saying you can't stand your car, your car could be stolen or just stop operating.

If you keep saying you're broke, guess what? You'll always be broke.

If you keep saying you can't trust a man or trust a woman, you will always find someone in your life to hurt and betray you.

If you keep saying you can't find a job, you will remain unemployed.

If you keep saying you can't find someone to love you or believe in you,

your very thought will attract more experiences to confirm your beliefs.

If you keep talking about a divorce or break up in a relationship, then you might end up with just that.

Turn your thoughts and conversations around to be more positive and power packed with faith, hope, love and action. Don't be afraid to believe that you can have what you want and what you deserve.

Watch your Thoughts, they become words.
Watch your words, they become actions
Watch your actions, they become habits.
Watch your Habits, they become character.
Watch your Character, for it becomes your Destiny

"For out of the abundance of the heart the mouth speaketh. A good man out of the good treasure of the hearth bringeth forth good things; and an evil man out of the evil treasure bringeth forth evil things. But I say unto you, that every idle word that men shall speak, they shall give account thereof in the day of judgment." Mathew 12:34-36

The minute you settle for less than you deserve, you get even less than you settle for. Speak positive things into your life. Your words can definitely decide your future. "If you control your tongue, you will speak blessings into your life."

Melvina Harrison

An Attitude of Gratitude

How many times do you say "Thank You", during the course of a day? From an early age, we were taught to always say, "thank you" when someone shows us kindness, be it a gift, a ride, a loan, a meal, or through kind words. Even today as adults we say, "thank you" to our elders, family, friends, co-workers, and even to people we do not know. We say, "thank you" when we are told, "you did a good job", "nice car", "nice suit", "nice tie", "I like your hat", "I enjoyed the cake you baked", "girl you know you sang that song", "you made my day", and the list could goes on and on. By doing so, we are displaying an attitude of gratitude or giving pleasure or contentment which is what God expects from us, as indicated in **EPHESIANS 5:20. "Giving thanks ALWAYS for ALL things unto God the Father in the name of our Lord Jesus Christ."**

As always, there are some doubting Thomas' that are reading this article and saying those examples are not what gratitude means. Well, let's appease those doubting Thomas' and define the word 'gratitude'. According to Wikipedia, "*Gratitude* is nothing more than a feeling of thankfulness and an act of appreciation for a benefit received when accepted with an assumption of good faith that the motivation of the benefactor is to afford pleasure or contentment."

Although gratitude can mean thankfulness or to respond to a favor we received, the meaning runs much deeper in true believers where our hearts are filled with gratitude for the many blessings that God gives, even when the blessings seem small to our many wants or because we are unable to see them. David is a prime example of how he exemplified an attitude of gratitude. David was most definitely a man after God's own heart. Even in trying times, David continued to praise God. His heart was full of praise to God because he was keenly aware of what God had done for him, and what God could do for him and his family. David became King, he did not come from royalty, he was the least in his family, and his family was last in his tribe. David even sinned; however, God's Grace restored him **(Psalm 34:1: 107:15).**

As a Christian, our daily walk should be to make every effort to be more thankful to Him and do our utmost to live up to the call given to us in **(Heb 13:15), "By Him therefore let us offer the sacrifice of praise to God continually, that is, the fruit of our lips giving thanks to his name."**

Let's not just give thanks on Thanksgiving Day and Christmas, but display a grateful heart each and every day to everyone – everyone includes your enemies, those that do not like you, and those that despise you and smear your name. But remember, **(I THESS. 5:18) "In everything give thanks, for this is the will of God in Christ Jesus for you." The NIV says, "Give thanks in all circumstances."** So we're not to give thanks for everything, perhaps, but in everything we can have a grateful heart. Join me, as we let our light shine and show our gratitude by praising God forever and ever **(Psalm 150).** Do you have an "Attitude of Gratitude?"

ATTITUDE: A Positive Thinker - **SEES** the invisible, **FEELS** the intangible, and **ACHIEVES** the impossible.

Melvina Harrison

WORK YOUR FAITH

Hebrews 11: 1 Now faith is the substance of things hoped for, the evidence of things not seen.

Hebrews 11: 6 But without faith it is impossible to please Him. For he that cometh to God must believe that He is, and that He is a rewarder of those who diligently seek Him.

We as Christians know that without faith it is impossible to please God. Since god has power over the entire universe and has created everything in the universe why is it that we cannot have faith in him? We all know that "faith commeth by hearing; hearing the word of God." And "we walk by faith not by sight". We've heard these scriptures over and over again. However we still lack in our faith. I believe it's impossible to please God without faith because that is a total insult to him. After he has proven himself over and over again. Why is it we still do not believe? We all know that the opposite of faith is "fear". And many times when we have doubt and fear in our hearts it is impossible to please God. "God is a rewarder to those who diligently seek him." So why do we lack in our faith?

Remember when Peter walked on the water? He was exercising his Faith in God. Remember the woman with the issue of Blood, who was healed just by touching Jesus's garment? She was exercising her faith in God. Remember Jarius the ruler, who came to Jesus and said, my daughter is dying, please come and heal her, so that she may live. And when Jesus went to his home, he healed the little girl and she lived. Jarius also was exercising his faith in God. I'm sure you may say, yeah, but that was in the bible days, faith doesn't work that way now. I say to you that it does work that way now. God is the same yesterday, today and forever more. His word is true and it shall not return void.

The difference with these people is that, "they worked their faith". The woman with the issue of Blood said to herself, "If I could just touch the hem of his garment I will be made whole." She crawled though crowds of people to get to Jesus. She could have been crushed to death by the throngs of people, or she could have just stayed at her house and prayed, "Please heal me Jesus". But she worked her faith, by taking the risk of death, just to touch the hem of his garment. "She worked her faith" Peter worked his faith by Stepping out onto the water. He also took a risk; a risk of drowning, but he stepped out and worked his faith. Jarius worked his faith also. He could have sent one of his servants to Jesus, because he was a wealthy man, but he worked his faith by going to Jesus himself.

James 2:26 For as the body without the spirit is dead, so faith without works is dead also.

To prove your faith in god here are some things you can do to exercise your faith:

THINK IT: Think about what God has promise you in his word. He is your heavenly father, that will give you anything you ask for.

TRUST IT: Trust God with all you heart, and lean not to your own understanding, and he will give you the desires of your heart.

TEST IT: Before Peter walked on the water, I'm sure he tested it first, however with such faith he began to walk without hesitation

TRY IT: God said prove me this day, and I will open the windows of heaven, and will pour you out a blessing that you will not have room enough to receive. That means blessing of prosperity in every area of your life.

If you really have Faith in God, I say to you , "Work you Faith, and it will Work for You."

Are You Flying with Eagles or Gobbling with Turkeys?

Many people don't realize that their fate as well as their destiny is proclaimed in the people they associate with. Your friends and associates can stimulate you to help you reach your highest potential or they can bring you down.

When we look as birds of the kingdom, we realize that there are significant differences in their lifestyle and associations. We've all heard that "Birds of a Feather Flock Together". That's absolutely the truth. And People in many ways are similar. We have a tendency to associate with people who make us feel good or people we are comfortable with, staying within "Our Comfort Zone". However, in order to reach your highest potential, you may have to remove yourself from your "Comfort Zone".

Let's take a look at two distinct Birds. The Eagle and the turkey, and examine how they live and communicate.

The eagle is recognized as the "king of birds"; by reason of his great size, his remarkable power of flight, and his keenness of vision. The Eagle also builds his home to heights where the atmosphere is always below freezing, and descend to the warm earth almost every day. They have great strength and can kill small mammals, large birds, etc., even though they never slay except to eat. The Eagle is also known to be an intelligent Bird and is our National Emblem.

Turkeys on the other hand are considered to be bird-brained. They are not as intelligent as the Eagle and in many cases will peck each other to death if they don't receive proper care. Turkeys can be downright mean at times and can drown in a rain storm. They hear the thunderstorm and usually look up with their mouths open, and after swallowing too much water, they drown.

There is a story about an American Indian who found an eagle's egg and put it into the nest of a prairie chicken. The eaglet hatched with the brood of chicks and grew up with them.

All its life, the changeling eagle, thought it was a prairie chicken, it did what the prairie chickens did. It scratched in the dirt for seeds and insects to eat. It clucked and cackled and flew in a brief thrashing of wings and flurry of feathers no more than a few feet off the ground. After all, that's how prairie chickens were supposed to fly.

Years passed and the changeling eagle grew very old. One day, it saw a magnificent bird far above in the cloudless sky, hanging with graceful majesty on the powerful wind currents, and it soared with scarcely a beat of its strong golden wings.

"What a beautiful bird!" said the changeling eagle to its neighbor. "What is it?" "That's an eagle - the chief of the birds," the neighbor clucked. "But don't give it a second thought. You could never be like him."

So the changeling eagle never gave it a second thought. Throughout its entire life the changeling eagle pride itself as being a prairie chicken and it died thinking it was a prairie chicken. (Story Taken From: The Christophers, Bits & Pieces)

Keep in mind that we have personal differences and very unique gifts that God has given us. And in order to soar like an eagle, we must surround ourselves with Positive experiences and Positive People. Of course, no one wants to end up like the "Eagle who thought he was a Chicken". Just as the Eagle, when placed in an inferior environment we become inferior. So not to be inferior or less than what we ought to be, it is imperative that we surround ourselves with people who can help us grow, stimulate us, point us in the right direction, help us up when we stumble, give us hope when we are down, and lead us to God when we are Godless.

At this point, say to yourself I will surround myself with Positive and encouraging people who can help me establish my Self Confidence and build my Self Esteem.

I leave you with a word of advice, never, never, never surround yourself with people that are negative, but instead make it a point to surround yourself with people who will encourage you to reach your Highest and Greatest Potential.

Now which do you prefer? Do you want to Soar like an eagle or gobble like a turkey?

CLEANING UP HOUSE

Last Week I threw out Bitterness
It was getting old and in the way.
It kept me from being kind to others,
I couldn't do things GOD's way.

I threw out unforgiveness,
it was crowding up my mind,
I had to make room for Love and Peace,
and Dreams of every kind.

I threw out a book on MY PAST
(didn't have time to read it anyway).
Replaced it with New Goals, New Dreams
And Started reading it today.

I threw out all my childhood fears,
because God told me so.
And Got me a NEW PHILOSOPHY and ,
Threw out the old one from long ago.

I Brought in some great books,
Called I Can, I Will, and I Must.
Threw out I might, I think and I ought.
And filled it with books of Faith, Love and Trust.

I ran across an OLD FRIEND,
Haven't seen him in a while.
For Jesus is his name
And I really like his style.

He also helped me to do some cleaning
And added some thing's Himself.
Like PRAYER, HOPE and FAITH,
Yes I placed them on the top shelf.

I picked up something special
And placed it at the door.
I FOUND IT - its called PEACE.
Because Nothing gets me down anymore.
Yes, I've got my house looking real nice.

Looks good around the place.
For things like Worry, Strife and Trouble
There just isn't any space.
It sure is good to do a little house cleaning,

Getting rid of the old things on the shelf.
It makes things look a lot brighter,
Maybe you should TRY IT FOR YOURSELF.

Melvina Harrison

Don't Look Back

But his wife looked back behind him, and she became a pillar of salt.
Genesis 19:26

Remember Lot's Wife? We don't really know much about her, except that when she turned around to look back at Sodom she turned into a Pillar of salt. The book of Genesis tells us what happened that day. While they were fleeing, she looked back to get one last glance and became a pillar of salt.

When she turned back to take that last look, she was being disobedient to God and it was clear that she didn't want to leave Sodom. She wanted to steal one last glance, and it cost her everything.

When Jesus said to His disciples " Remember Lot's wife' " (Luke 17:32), it was a warning not to look back. When we look back it gives the devil a chance to remind us of how it used to be. Let's face it, we've all had some fun times when we were in the world. And the devil reminds us of the fun times. However, he doesn't remind us of when we were miserable and empty; lonely and terrified of life as well as death. " Why was looking back such a horrible sin causing the judgment of God to fall upon Lot's wife? When all she did was steal a quick glance. But it wasn't just one last look. It was a lingering desire to stay there. You see, looking back is a step toward going back.

When we look back:

- It hinders our growth with God.
- It builds frustration, depression, and bitterness.
- It slows down progress, because when we constantly look back we can't move forward.
- It harbors unforgiveness.
- It allows us to carry a lot of "Extra Baggage".

Melvina Harrison

That is why Jesus said, " 'No one, having put his hand to the plow, and looking back, is fit for the kingdom of God' " (Luke 9:62). If you are going to follow Christ, you need to look forward, not over your shoulder. Remember Lot's wife: you don't want to be turned into a pillar of salt.

Go Where You're Celebrated; Not Where you're Tolerated!!!

Matthew 10:14
And whosoever shall not receive you, nor hear your words, when ye depart out of that house or city, shake off the dust from your feet.

Most people will not appreciate your gifts, talents and unique abilities. Don't be surprised and don't be alarmed if they don't give you the time of day. However, there will be a unique moment in time when God will cause a divine relationship to occur with someone who will actually share and admire your uniqueness. And when you cross paths with this person who celebrates your gifts, take heed to what they say, because it can affect your destiny.

Most people who don't celebrate you are already fixated on realizing their own dreams; and they are trying to establish their own uniqueness. Therefore they are fully engaged with themselves. When you meet the right person to connect with they will cause you to shine and help you establish what God has created you to become.

Listed below are several secrets that you must do in order to establish your dreams:

1. Go where you are celebrated; not where you're tolerated.

When Jesus visited his own home town, the people did not receive him. Maybe because he was the carpenter's son; or maybe because they knew his family history. Nevertheless, because of their lack of faith in him, he could not perform any miracles there. Of course they should have respected him simply because he was one of them. But many times when people know something about you and where you come from, they have a tendency not to believe in you. Unbelief is the greatest hindrance to God's favor. Therefore, if others do not respect you or have faith in you, move on!

Remember oranges don't grow in Alaska. If you want to grow oranges, try Florida or California. Likewise you must be planted in an environment and climate conducive to your personal growth and enrichment. Go where you are celebrated, and not merely tolerated.

2. Go the extra mile.

Stand tall and separate yourself from the crowd. Don't be like everybody else. Break the mold. God has created an original design in you. So lift up your head and throw your shoulders back and be the Best that God has created you to be. By going the extra mile and exceeding your potential you will show yourself and others that you are a true asset and somebody will eventually take notice.

3. Replace anxiety with creativity.

Philippians 4:6 Be anxious for nothing, but in everything by prayer and supplication, with thanksgiving, let your requests be made known to God;

Don't be overly anxious. Anxiety drains you of your energy and immobilizes your resourcefulness. Get a grip on yourself and patiently possess your goal. Be more childlike, playful, and humorous. See things differently. Consider all of your options. Prayerfully and skillfully evaluate the best alternatives available for you to determine the most appropriate course of action to take.

4. Guard your tongue and flourish where you are planted

Although you may see some things happening to other people. That doesn't mean you need to say anything negative about it. Remember we are all constantly growing and maturing in our everyday lives. Change can come to all of us. Earn the right to be heard by giving your contributions and by showing that you are a team player; in your job; in your family; and in your church. Once people feel how much you care, they will take interest in how much you know. Remember, it's better to make friends, and not enemies.

5. Don't sweat the small stuff

Don't let trivial things irritate you, and distract you from your vision. Sometimes it's the small stuff that can be most aggravating. It's easier to dodge a rock than if someone were to come up and throw sand in your eyes. The smallest of things sometimes can be the most hindering. Avoid negative conversations and complaining around others. Be productive and focus on the future. If you stay on track in your journey, you'll get there. Tune out the small stuff that comes to distract you from your dream, and face things with a positive attitude.

6. Follow your instincts

You don't necessarily have to know what's going to happen; how it's going to happen; or when it's going to happen. Just establish what you want and make it happen. Therefore be led by your gut instincts. Intuitively, you know what you want to do. So stop questioning yourself and stop being double minded about it. Trust your internal knowledge and move on them! When you do this you create what you want to happen in your world.

7. Remember the future is in you – not in them

Contrary to popular belief, your future is not predicated on others. Your future lies within you. With God on your side you can accomplish anything. You can excel and make your dreams come true. When you are firm and solid in your convictions, you can bring about your own destiny. Never underestimate the power of God to help fulfill your destiny. When you put your trust in God anything is possible. So continue to believe in yourself and make your dreams come true. But most of all, "Go where you're celebrated, and Not Merely Tolerated"!

Melvina Harrison

Psalms 23 (For the Work Place)

The Lord is my real boss, and I shall not want.

He gives me peace and serenity, when chaos is all around me.

He restores my sole and gently reminds me to pray and do all things *Without Murmuring and Complaining.*

He reminds me that he is my source, and not my job.

He restores my soul and sanity everyday and guides my decisions that I might honor him in all I do.

Even though I face adversity; absurd amounts of e-mails; system

crashes; unrealistic deadlines; budget cuts; gossiping

co-workers; discriminating supervisors and an aging body

that doesn't cooperate with me every morning; I still will not stop---

for the Lord is with me!

His presence, His peace, and His power

will continue to restore me and see me through.

He raises me up; even when they fail to promote me.

He claims me as His own; even when the company threatens to let me go.

His Faithfulness and love is better than any bonus check.

His retirement plan beats every 401k there is!

When it's all said and done, I will dwell in the house of the Lord and continue to work for him forever and ever.

Which means I'll be working for God a whole lot longer than this Job;

and for that, I BLESS HIS NAME!!! AMEN!!

Renew Your Mind with Seven Principles to Successful Networking

Networking is an important element in any business or career. Networking could help you meet that person who could elevate your career to the next level. In this section I will address seven principles to successful networking. I call them the seven P's.

1. **Be Professional:** *(The bible says, "Let everything be decent and in order")*

   *As a Professional, in any walk in life, always put your "Best Foot forward". People remember you if you Dress professional, Act professional and have a professional attitude. This is called the "Halo Effect". Let's think about this for a moment, when you do well in specific areas or present yourself in a professional manner, some people will remember you for those attributes and each time someone thinks of you or someone calls your name, they think of you as a "**True Professional**".*

   ➢ **Appearance** is very important. No matter what kind of job you have or where you work you should always **Dress** properly. Being neat and clean is a subset of dressing properly and maintaining a professional appearance. Never, ever forget that people will remember how you look as well as how you dress. "You never get a second chance to make a first impression"; therefore, seize the moment.

➢ Maximize every "**per chance**" meeting. Place yourself in opportunities for giving out your business card because you never know who you might meet. If you do not have your own personal business card it is essential for successful networking that you take the time to have your own **Business Cards** printed. We all know that business cards are not inexpensive so if you cannot afford to purchase business cards, print them out yourself using your own personal computer using appropriate paper. As you give your card out remember to ask that person for their business card in return and follow up on that lead.

2. Be polite:

➢ Always politely introduce yourself to people even if you met them previously. Do not have people trying to guess your name because that is an insult to you and to them. Properly introduce yourself and tell them where and when you met the last time.

➢ Never be rude, **rudeness** is not the "In Thing" any more. People will appreciate your politeness. If the person is talking with someone else, wait in the background until they have finished, then politely approach them.

3. Be Pleasant:

➢ People do not have time for boring conversations. Learn to read body language. Many times people are ready to move onto the next person and next conversation. **Know** when to let go.

4. Be positive:

➢ Negative vibes, are a **No Go**. Be positive at all times. Busy people do not have time to hear your whining and complaining about something or some one else.

5. Presentation

➢ Your **presentation** is very important. Present yourself as a professional. People have sized you up and formed an opinion of you in the first 3-5 seconds of meeting them. So always tailor your presentation with a positive impact/spin.

6. Take the Plunge

➢ "If you **play it safe** in life, you've decided that you don't want to grow any more."

➢ – Shirley Hufstedler, First U.S. Secretary of Education, 1979-1981

> Life is too important to play it safe. Be willing to take a **Risk** in every thing you do. Your destiny depends on you taking a chance. An example -- if you have never been embarrassed or you have never met someone you do not know this is perceived as playing your life too safe. Step outside of your safety zone and take the plunge in order to network successfully.

7. **Pray.**

> Finally **Pray**. Prayer changes things and we should always pray without ceasing. In everything through Prayer and Supplication make your request know unto God.

Finally, if you follow these **seven principles to successful networking**, your music career or any chosen career or path you choose will undoubtedly "Prove to be very Promising".

CHRISTIAN VALUES TO LIVE BY

As an instructor for the Army, I am constantly reminded of the Army's Core Values, which is the acronym for Leadership (LDRSHIP).

L=Loyalty
D=Duty
R=Respect
S=Selfless-Service
H=Honor
I=Integrity
P=Personal Courage

As a Christian I am also reminded of the values that God want us to live by. God expects us to walk in his wisdom and represent him in everything we do. Here is a list of Ten values that are emphasized strongly in the Bible, that we as Christians should live by.

1. Worship only God

One day, a religious leader asked Jesus which of the commandments was most important:

> **"The most important one" answered Jesus, "is this: 'Hear, O Israel, the Lord our God, the Lord is one. Love the Lord your God with all your heart and with all your soul and with all your mind and with all your strength.' (NIV, Mark 12:28-30)**

2. Respect all people

After saying "Love the Lord your God" is the most important of the commandments, Jesus continued,

> **The second is this: 'Love your neighbor as yourself.' There is no commandment greater than these." (NIV, Mark 12:31)**

The English word "love" has many different meanings, but the Greek word, *agape*, used in the New Testament, is commonly known as "Christian love." It means respect, affection, benevolence, good-will and concern for the welfare of the one loved.In His *Parable of the Good Samaritan*, Jesus made the point that we should extend our Christian love to **all** people of the world, regardless of race, religion, nationality or any other artificial distinction. We must practice that Christian love even toward our enemies! (Matthew 5:43-48)

Jesus' Golden Rule is, "Do unto others as you would have them do unto you." We should not say or do anything unless we can answer "Yes" to the question, "Would I want that said or done to me?" Neither should we fail to do the good things we would expect of others.

3. Be humble

Humility or being humble is a quality of being courteously respectful of others. It is the opposite of aggressiveness, arrogance, boastfulness, and vanity. Acting with humility does not in any way deny our own self worth. Rather, it affirms the inherent worth of all persons. Humility is exactly what is needed to live in peace and harmony with all persons. It dissipates anger and heals old wounds. It allows us to see the dignity and worth of all God's people. Humility distinguishes the wise leader from the arrogant power-seeker (Proverbs 17:7, Matthew 20:20-28).

4. Be honest

Honesty and integrity are held as very important values throughout the Bible, and any deception to gain an advantage or harm another is prohibited by the Ten Commandments (Exodus 20:16) and other Bible passages. Deception may be by false statements, half-truths, innuendo, or failing to tell the whole truth. It is all too common in advertising, business dealings, politics and everyday life. We must strongly resist the temptation to engage in any form of theft, cheating, deception, innuendo, slander or gossip.

5. Live a moral life

Do you not know that your body is a temple of the Holy Spirit, who is in you, whom you have received from God? You are not your own; you were bought at a price. Therefore honor God with your body. (NIV, 1 Corinthians 6:19-20)

Jesus gave a list of actions that constitute immoral uses of the body: evil thoughts, murder, adultery, sexual immorality, theft, false testimony, slander, greed, malice, deceit, lewdness, envy, arrogance and foolishness. The apostle Paul gave similar lists.

We often think of morality in terms of sexual sins, but according to Jesus, sins such as slander, greed, deceit, and arrogance are equally immoral.

6. Be generous with time and money

The Bible tells us to share generously with those in need, and good things will come to us in turn. Each of us has something to offer to someone in need. We can give our money and our time to charity, be a friend to someone who is sick or lonely, do volunteer work or choose a service-oriented occupation. We may give unselfishly of our time to our spouse, children or parents.

7. Practice what you preach; don't be a hypocrite

If there was any one group of people that Jesus couldn't stand, it was hypocrites! The Pharisees of Jesus' time were a religious and political party that insisted on very strict observance of Biblical laws on tithing, ritual purity and other matters. At the same time, many of the Pharisees forgot the true spirit and intent of the law and became self-indulgent, self-righteous, snobbish, and greedy. That led Jesus to remarks such as,

> **Woe to you, teachers of the law and Pharisees, you hypocrites! You are like whitewashed tombs, which look beautiful on the outside but on the inside are full of dead men's bones and everything unclean. In the same way, on the outside you appear to people as righteous but on the inside you are full of hypocrisy and wickedness.** *(NIV, Matthew 23:27-28)*

8. Don't be self-righteous

No one is perfect; we are all sinners in one way or another (Romans 3:23). Living a moral life means taking responsibility for controlling **our own** behavior. If we say or even think we are better than people we consider to be "sinners," we are guilty of the sin of self-righteousness. It is not our right to look down on, criticize, judge or try to control other people; judgment is to be left to God. Jesus said,

> **Do not judge, so that you may not be judged. For with the judgment you make you will be judged, and the measure you give will be the measure you get. Why do you see the speck in your neighbor's eye, but do not notice the log in your own eye? Or how can you say to your neighbor, 'Let me take the speck out of your eye,' while the log is in your own eye? You hypocrite, first take the log out of your own eye, and**

then you will see clearly to take the speck out of your neighbor's eye.
(NRSV, Matthew 7:1-5)

9. Don't hold a grudge

Jesus said there is no place for hatred, holding a grudge, revenge, retaliation or getting even in the life of a Christian:

You have heard that it was said, 'Eye for eye, and tooth for tooth.' But I tell you, Do not resist an evil person. If someone strikes you on the right cheek, turn to him the other also. And if someone wants to sue you and take your tunic, let him have your cloak as well. *(NIV, Matthew 5:38-40)*

You have heard that it was said, 'Love your neighbor and hate your enemy.' But I tell you: Love your enemies and pray for those who persecute you, that you may be sons of your Father in heaven. He causes his sun to rise on the evil and the good, and sends rain on the righteous and the unrighteous. *(NIV, Matthew 5:43-45)*

Bearing a grudge and seeking revenge are ***never*** appropriate responses to a perceived wrong. A grudge destroys the grudge-holder with bitterness, and revenge only escalates hostilities. Jesus told us we must reconcile with our adversaries, forgive their transgressions, and let go of the anger that may tempt us to commit an act of revenge.

10. Forgive others

If you forgive those who sin against you, your heavenly Father will forgive you. But if you refuse to forgive others, your Father will not forgive your sins. (NLT, Matthew 6:14-15) God is merciful and forgives our sins and failings. In the same way, we must be merciful and forgive other people who sin against us or do us harm.

Melvina Harrison

TEN COMMANDMENTS FOR A POSITIVE WORK ENVIRONMENT

1. Know your job well, and know that God has anointed you for that position. God uses ordinary people and ordinary circumstances as a training ground to perfect our character. Even if you think you're not qualified for that position, God has already qualified you.

2. Don't expect every one on the job to appreciate you. God values what you do and he values your humility. Some people just won't understand how you got the position you're in; and because of that some people won't appreciate you or respect your position. However, God appreciates you, and that's all you need.

3. Embrace all opportunities for change and promotion. As we reach the stage of maturity when we are no longer surprised by change; many people will fall by the wayside because they are not willing to change. If we never change, we never grow. Change is good. It allows us to progress to the next level in our lives.

Psalm 75:6-7

6 For promotion cometh neither from the east, nor from the west, nor from the south.

7 But God is the judge: he putteth down one, and setteth up another.

4. Do your job well and continue to remember the vision. The secret to performing your duties well where you are is to maintain a vision of where you're headed.

Proverbs 29:17-18

Where there is no vision, the people perish: but he that keepeth the law, happy is he.

5. Don't let the work environment get inside you. To counter bad attitudes, behavior, and gossip, maintain a regular diet of prayer and Bible study. Keep the righteousness of God inside of you.

Matthew 5:9

Blessed are the peacemakers: for they shall be called the children of God.

6. Increase your capacity and enthusiasm to work with people who have difficult personalities. Too often we only try to fit in and connect with others similar to us. God may have put you in that position to minister to those with difficult personalities. Treat them with kindness, you will receive your reward.

7. Where you are now is not where you are going to be in the future. Be peaceful while progressing toward the higher call.

8. Achieve phenomenal results with minimal confusion. We spend too much time trying to compensate for our weaknesses rather than capitalizing on our strengths.

9. Do not pledge to be apart of cliques and groups. The enemy tempts us with the security of the group and the approval of others.

10. Keep a song in your heart each day. Spend time with God and in his presence. Study His Word, offer up prayer, and look deep inside yourself to call up your song—praise and worship Him daily.

Psalm 98:1

O sing unto the LORD a new song; for he hath done marvelous things: his right hand, and his holy arm, hath gotten him the victory.

Keep Your Dream Alive

Genesis 37:5 – 8 Joseph had a dream, and when he told his brothers about it, they hated him even more. 37:6 He said to them, "Listen to this dream I had: 37:7 There we were, binding sheaves of grain in the middle of the field. Suddenly my sheaf rose up and stood upright and your sheaves surrounded my sheaf and bowed down to it!" 37:8 Then his brothers asked him, "Do you really think you will rule over us or have dominion over us?" They hated him even more because of his dream and because of what he said.

God places inside each of us a Dream that will soon come to pass. Your dreams are born inside of you; you already have what it takes to establish your dreams; and God will instill a hunger inside you to require you to accomplish your Dream. Dreams always require Nurturing, Energy, Faith and Focus.

In order to accomplish your dreams that have been placed in your heart, here are several steps you must follow to make your dreams come true.

1. ***Recognize that your dream comes from God.*** James 1:17 says, "Every good and perfect gift comes from God".

2. ***Make sure your Dream is in alignment with God and not contrary to God's Law.*** Your mind must be at peace for your greatest ideas to flow. Greatnesses grow best in the soil of peace.

3. ***Believe in your Dream.*** Believe in yourself and believe that God has given you a dream, to fulfill his purpose and to glorify him. Therefore, he will give you the plan and the provisions to accomplish your dream.

4. ***Have Faith and Focus on your dream.*** Have the faith to believe that God is not a man that he should lie. What ever he told you

will happen, and it shall come to pass. He is true to his promises. Focus on people that can help you accomplish your dream. People who are for you and not against you. Contrary to popular belief, everyone will not believe in your dream; or want you to succeed.

5. ***Announce your Dream To Others.*** Something remarkable happens, when we boldly announce our dreams out loud. It lights the fire inside of us; it illuminates that desire in us and gives us confidents to move obstacles out of our way. When you announce your dream, your enemies will be exposed. Those who oppose you will be forced to expose themselves. Then you will know who is for you, or against you.

6. ***Your Dream may intimidate those who are closest to you.*** Your dream is yours alone. Others do no see what you see, or feel what you feel. So you can't expect them understand the joy that is in your heart. Even those who are closest to you may feel intimidated by your dream. When Joseph told his brothers about his dream, they became angry with him and set out to kill him in order to destroy his dream. Many times people will misread you or misunderstand you, because they feel uncomfortable about your dream.

7. ***Keep your Fire burning.*** Take the time to refuel your dreams, ignite the fire insider of you. Talk about it with others who believe in you. Associate with people who are for you and who can assist you in accomplishing your dream. And most of create a plan that will help you accomplish your dream. If you remember these few steps you can accomplish your dream and make it happen. Keep Your Dream Alive!!

Be Encouraged

If you are finding yourself discouraged, read the story of Joseph that chronicles his trials and tribulations and ultimately his victory that God had promised him since childhood. If you are finding yourself in an impossible situation, read the story of Abraham and Sarah who at the age of ninety was promised by God to bear a child to fulfill God's promise to Abraham that he would be a father of many nations. If the enemy has been fighting you, read the story of David who slew the giant Goliath with an exact pinpointed throw from his slingshot.

Stories of victory and triumph are made available to us so that we might be strengthened and encouraged to continue on. (Genesis 37-48) (Genesis 17:15-22) (1 Samuel 17:4-57)

Be encouraged to read your Bible and receive the blessings that flow throughout its timeless pages.

Read and meditate on these scriptures:

Joshua 1:8 "This book of the law shall not depart out of thy mouth; but thou shalt meditate therein day and night, that thou mayest observe to do according to all that is written therein: for then thou shalt make thy way prosperous, and then thou shalt have good success."

Psalm 119:10-16 "With my whole heart have I sought Thee: O let me not wander from Thy commandments. Thy word have I hid in mine heart, that I might not sin against Thee. Blessed art Thou, O LORD: teach me Thy statutes. With my lips have I declared all the judgments of Thy mouth. I have rejoiced in the way of Thy testimonies, as much as in all riches. I will meditate in Thy precepts, and have respect unto Thy ways. I will delight myself in Thy statutes: I will not forget Thy word."

James 1:22-25 "But be ye doers of the word, and not hearers only, deceiving your own selves. For if any be a hearer of the word, and not a doer, he is like unto a man beholding his natural face in a glass: For he beholdeth himself, and goeth his way, and straightway forgetteth what manner of man he was. But whoso looketh into the perfect law of liberty, and continueth therein, he being not a forgetful hearer, but a doer of the work, this man shall be blessed in his deed."

Psalm 37:3-6 "Trust in the LORD, and do good; so shalt thou dwell in the land, and verily thou shalt be fed. Delight thyself also in the LORD; and He shall give thee the desires of thine heart. Commit thy way unto the LORD; trust also in Him; and He shall bring it to pass. And He shall bring forth thy righteousness as the light, and thy judgment as the noonday."

All of these scriptures can be found in the King James Bible.

So be encouraged and seek God and his holy word today.

"We are what we repeatedly do.
Excellence, then is not an act, but a habit." -Aristotle

TEN RULES FOR STAYING YOUNG:

1. Throw out nonessential numbers. This includes age, weight, and height. Let the doctor worry about them. That is why you pay him/her.

2. Keep only cheerful friends. The grouches pull you down. If you really need a grouch, there are probably a few dozen of your relatives to do the job.

3. Keep learning. Learn more about the Bible, computer, crafts, gardening, whatever. Just never let the brain stay idle.

4. Laugh often, long and loud. Laugh until you gasp for breath. Laugh so much that you can be tracked in the store by your distinctive laughter.

5. Do not worry about situations beyond your control. God is still on His throne!

6. The tears happen. Endure, grieve, and move on. The only person who is with us our entire lives, is ourselves.

7. Surround yourself with what you love, whether it is family, pets, keepsakes, music, plants, hobbies, whatever. Your home is your refuge.

8. Cherish your health. If it is good, preserve it. If it is unstable, improve it. If it is beyond what you can improve, get help.

9. Don't take guilt trips. Shoulder only your own responsibilities. Then go to the mall, the next county, a foreign country, but not to guilt. God forgives and forgets. Go to Him.

10. Tell the people you love that you love them, at every opportunity.

Remember, life is not measured by the number of breaths we take, but by the moments that take our breath away.

WORDS OF WISDOM

1. Love starts with a smile, grows with a kiss, and ends with a tear.

2. Don't cry over anyone who won't cry over you.

3. If love isn't a game, why are there so many players?

4. Good friends are hard to find, harder to leave, and impossible to forget.

5. You can only go as far as you push.

6. Actions speak louder than words.

7. The hardest thing to do is watch the one you love, love somebody else.

8. Don't let the past hold you back; you're missing the good stuff.

9. Life is short. If you don't look around once in a while, you might miss it.

10. A best friend is like a four leaf clover: hard to find and lucky to have.

11. If you think that the world means nothing, think again. You might mean the world to someone else.

12. Best friends can last forever.

13. When it hurts to look back, and you're scared to look ahead, you can look beside you and your best friend will be there.

14. True friendship never ends.

15. Friends are forever.

16. Good friends are like stars. You don't always see them, but you know they are always there.

17. Don't frown. You never know who is falling in love with your smile.

18. What do you do when the only person who can make you stop crying is the person who made you cry?

19. Nobody is perfect until you fall in love with them.

20. Everything is okay in the end. If it's not okay, then it's not the end.

21. Most people walk in and out of your life. But only friends leave footprints in your heart.

QUESTIONS FOR REFLECTION
"GET INTO POSITION TO BE BLESSED"
CHAPTER 1, PAGE 1

1. *Are you taking Responsibility for your own Success and Blessings?*

2. *What are some ways you can "Get Into Position To Be Blessed"?*

3. *Do You want to help others be successful and become Blessed? How can that help you on your road to success?*

4. *What does God mean in Deuteronomy 28:11-13, when he said, "the fruit of your body will be blessed"? "He will bless all the work of your hand"? "You shall lend to many nations, but you shall not borrow"? "And the LORD will make you the head and not the tail; you shall be above only, and not be beneath"?*

QUESTIONS FOR REFLECTION
"RENEW YOUR MIND AND BE BLESSED"
CHAPTER 2, PAGE 6

1. Is it true that the mind controls our thoughts and actions? Can we improve our thoughts to be positive?

2. The Bible also says in Phil. 4:8 - "Whatever is true, right, pure...let your mind dwell on these things...." What does that mean to you? How can we improve our thoughts if we "Set our mind on things above"?

3. Can the mind play tricks on us? How? How can the mind keep us from being successful?

4. Share your thoughts as how "controlling your mind" has increased your positive behavior.

Questions for Reflection
"The Power Of The Tongue"
Chapter 3, page 10

1. The Bible says, "Death and Life are in the power of the tongue: and they that love it shall eat the fruit thereof." Proverbs 18:21. What does that mean to you? Can we speak things into existence? How?

2. Can our tongue be a blessing or a curse to us? Can it also be a blessing or a curse to our friends and family? How?

3. Why does the Bible tell us to tame the tongue?

4. Can someone be hurt or offended, if we don't tame the tongue? How?

QUESTIONS FOR REFLECTION
"AN ATTITUDE OF GRATITUDE"
CHAPTER 4, PAGE 13

1. (I THESS. 5:18) "In everything give thanks, for this is the will of God in Christ Jesus for you." The bible says we should give thanks in all circumstances. Why is that important? Should we give thanks, even in times of trouble?

2. How can your Attitude, show Gratitude?

3.   When we give thanks to others, is that a good way to build relations?

4. Can your attitude of gratitude affect how others believe in Jesus Christ? Can having a poor attitude affect others beliefs?

QUESTIONS FOR REFLECTION
"WORK YOUR FAITH"
CHAPTER 5, PAGE 17

1. Hebrews 11: 1 Now faith is the substance of things hoped for, the evidence of things not seen.   How can we believe in something, that we have not seen?

2. Hebrews 11: 6 But without faith it is impossible to please Him. For he that cometh to God must believe that He is, and that He is a rewarder of those who diligently seek Him.   Why is it impossible to please God, without faith?

3. The Bible says, "if you only have faith the size of a mustard see, you can move mountains". What does that mean? Is faith important to have even in troubled times? Why?

4. What are some ways you can "Work Your Faith"?

QUESTIONS FOR REFLECTION
"ARE YOU FLYING WITH EAGLES OR GOBBLING WITH TURKEYS"
CHAPTER 6, PAGE 19

1. How can your destiny be defined by who you associate with?

2. Is it important to associate with people who are for you or against you?

3. Can people in high positions influence you to reach your highest potential? How?

4. What happens when we associate with people who don't have high standards? Or Dreams and Goals?

QUESTIONS FOR REFLECTION
"CLEANING UP HOUSE"
CHAPTER 7, PAGE 22

1.   Explain how, cleaning up your own feelings of bitterness and unforgiveness can help you? Can it also help others around you?

2. Why does bitterness and unforgiveness weigh us down?

3. Is it healthy to forgive? Why is it unhealthy not to forgive?

4. Who do you need to forgive today? Why?

Questions for Reflection
"Don't Look Back"
Chapter 8, page 25

1. How does looking back on past mistakes discourage you? How can it help you?

2. If God tells you Not to look back at your Past, should you be obedient? Why?

3. What are some things you can tell someone else, when their past is holding them back? How can you encourage them to look forward and "press towards a higher call"?

Questions for Discussion
"Go Where You're Celebrated, Not Where You're Tolerated"

1. Do you celebrate yourself? Do you celebrate others? Why?

What does the Bible say about celebrating others?

3. If someone doesn't respect you or celebrate you, what must you do? What does Jesus tell his disciples to do?

NOTES

NOTES

NOTES

NOTES

NOTES

NOTES